# SNITCHING

## GUIDE TO HOW IT GOES DOWN

# MS. TEE

**ROYAL-T
PUBLISHING**

ISBN: 978-0-578-51515-1

ROYAL-T PUBLISHING
P.O Box 600
New York, NY 10030
Email: Royaltypub@gmail.com

Instagram: @harlem_heroine

Snitching Credits:
Written by: Ms Tee
Cover Concept: Tonia Taylor

# ACKNOWLEDGMENTS

S HOUT OUT TO an OG who pushed me to make this happen. We've been like family for over 30 years and the love has never wavered.

This is something that the streets needed, and I made it happen. Shout out to those who gave me their information in order to make sure these stories were told.

Thank you, Wayne Green aka Bump, for giving me the information I needed. Keep ya head up Boss. You're one of the great ones who inspired this book along with the Big homie OG Tommy Frost.

Thank you, Albert aka Alpo, for telling me your truth. Thanks for trusting me enough and allowing me into your world. You were a good sport and I appreciate your cooperation-no pun intended.

Thanks to my guy "Anonymous" for giving me your views. You are my guy. Much love.

Thanks to all that gave me their love and support. I am overwhelmed by the love that you all have shown me on my first book **Harlem Heroin(e).**

I am so thankful to all the people that entrusted me to get the information out as if there was no one else that could do it better. Thanks for recognizing an honorable woman when you see one.

**A True G**
**Ms. Tee**

# INTRODUCTION

THIS BOOK IS not being written to glorify the street life in no way shape or form. Selling drugs, murder and committing other crimes are wrong. Those of us who've done it and are still doing it should use this book as a learning tool.

This book is to provoke thought. We always ask – **"Why do the crime if you can't do the time?"** Well the answer isn't as easy as one might think.

This book is for those who are still in the game and may be faced with doing prison time at some point. The question to them is; Are you ready for the consequences?

Everyone isn't built for the game, so why play. Prison or death (unless you're lucky) has been and will always be the outcome of the game. Plain & Simple. Nothing has changed.

Choosing the game comes with rules that you are expected to abide by. Right?

Someone recently asked me; **Who made the rules? Are there really rules to the Game? Where are these rules written? Who's the author?** Great questions for which I have no answers for.

This book is told from an objective point of view although at times I will be subjective. It has been edited many times over due to the climate of the streets at this present time. So many things have occurred while I was writing this book, which is why I chose to be unbiased.

This book is about "**Snitching- The Guide to how it goes down**".

# CONTENTS

# SNITCHING

**S**NITCHING- WE HEAR this term being used more and more these days. We already know what it means. The question is, why do individuals **choose** to be in the game knowing what the consequences could be but decide to snitch on others as their way out.

"**Snitch**" meaning "informer" is indeed an older word, dating back to the late 18th century.

So, as we can see snitching started centuries ago with words like "infomah" (informer) as my fellow Jamaicans would say. The question will always remain the same "Why become a snitch? Some will say Why not. Fundamentally, it's just the easy way out. The

11

price that one is willing to pay in order not to fight or stand up can be very hefty. Why would a man want to be ridiculed and looked down upon for doing such a thing? How does a man potentially put himself and his family in danger by committing an act that at times warrants death by those that despise such behavior? There may be a few answers to that. Maybe he wants to be with his family and doesn't care what the world thinks. Maybe he just doesn't want to do the time. Everybody is not mentally ready to hear twenty-five to life or natural life in prison. If you say you are, you're lying. This doesn't mean you won't stand tall and do your time. I'm saying that no one is in the game saying, "I'm saving this money so I can go in and do these 25 years to life." Who willingly wants to lose that much time away from loved ones and life period?

As you will see, I will mention "Man" or "Men" a lot. I must admit that more men have become snitches than any woman in the history of snitching. This is a fact. You can also argue that more men have been in the game than there are women. That's a fair statement as well, but there is no denying that there has been and will always be a woman that has been there by that man's side who was probably running the operation as well, not to mention that probably got caught up too and never muttered a single word.

There are a lot of women that are doing time and have done time because men have snitched on them. These same women have held it down by doing their time and never said a word. They've given the system many years of their lives all because a "MAN' and sometimes it was their own man who they laid down with so lovingly every night and took care of who were the ones that betrayed them.

The thought of not going to jail or doing little jail time seems to outweigh, thoughts of sustaining integrity, loyalty, and even the safety of one's own family. How could a man sacrifice his family's safety to be free from something that he's guilty of? If we choose to be in it, we choose the ups the downs and all the risks. Right?

No matter what business we choose to be in, we must be very careful when it comes time to pick business partners and associates. No business can really run itself and one person can't run his own business without being able to have someone he can trust. When it comes to the streets it's the same thing. There is always going to be someone that knows what you're doing. You can't be the boss, the vendor, and the worker. It doesn't work like that. If so, that would be as the young kids say "Gucci". Then you wouldn't have to worry about no one taking you under because it's just YOU.

Murderers, drug dealers, thieves and legit business owners alike would love to have a trustworthy right-hand man/woman and they must be chosen carefully. It would be nice to be able to handle business all on your own, but the reality is that no matter what organization you run, or empire you build there must be individuals appointed to do certain tasks to get the job done. As the boss you don't always have to tell people everything that you do. It just helps to know someone has your back that is loyal and will go through the fire and get burned for you, and with you.

This book will show you the dilemma that the streets put many in. But was it the game, or were these individuals not what they portrayed to be? What about the justice system? Are they not to blame? They are the ones who come up with these great opportunities like this-

**COPS**- *"Well we know you killed 12 people, but we really want him over there for all the heroin and cocaine he's putting in the streets.*

**SUSPECT**- *"Hmmmm. So, although I committed multiple murders and should be facing the death penalty, I can go free one day if I give him up?*

Who wouldn't give this deal some thought? Don't lie to yourself. I see a whole lot of dudes taking that deal. I'm just saying. Now back to the justice system. Are they not at fault? They are the ones who've created this madness. They have total control over this epidemic of snitching. Cops are letting murderers come home but giving drug dealers life in prison. Think about that. The justice system sucks. Are drugs more important that human lives that have been taken senselessly?

There are a lot of people out here yelling that "**NO SNITCHING**" phrase and I agree to an extent. Some might say, unless you've been in that position you will never know what some have endured mentally to get to that point of "*telling*" until you are put in that same situation. I'm not in no way shape or form saying what they've done was right at all, but at some point, I must play the devil's advocate. Like I said in my first book, some of us never know how strong we are or aren't until shit really hits the fan; and that is a fair statement.

Did you know that the guy that created the "**NO SNITCHING**" campaign back in the day and wrote books became an informant himself? When asked what happened to his campaign, he said *"Man that was all to make money, fuck that. I had to do what I had to do."* Now ain't that some shit. Think about it. He got all of you out here running a campaign that he started and then turned his back on. Not to mention made tons of money from as well.

I'm sure some of you will be reading your own story from the outside looking in. For those of you that snitched some people may say that you've taken a very selfish approach. I say that a few of you took this way out under very unnecessary circumstances. If you get caught for anything and can't do at least 5 to 10 years that's a problem. Those of you who got caught up and snitched on a man or woman that had absolutely no dealings with you or your case, that is totally unacceptable. That's just my opinion.

What controls the mindset of a snitch? Is it fear? Is it jealousy? Is it one's own discontent? What would make a man say to himself; *"I'm not doing this time for what I know I did wrong, but instead I know some dirt on another man that will put him away for a lifetime, just so I can be free despite all of my wrong doings"*. Many times, this is the thought of an individual who hasn't even been propositioned yet. Why would one consider this as an option?

For the record, I am in no way promoting snitching, violence or the selling of drugs of any kind. The reality is that the streets and whatever is left of it will always be a way of life for some of you. It's unfortunate, but it's the truth. The lack of education, knowledge, motivation and ambition is the reason for not being able to progress.

Before I really get into it, let me distinguish being a snitch from being a witness or a victim once again. Whether some of you agree with this or not, it's the truth. Just grab a dictionary. Some of you are sending the wrong message to the youth. And then some of you grown ass men are just being ignorant to what's the truth.

This is what I was told by a NYC Police Detective and I agree. If an average working person sees someone shooting wildly into a crowd of men and your sister, brother or even an innocent child was shot and maybe even killed, they are a **witness** to a crime. If you are a civilian who works, and you are not in no way shape or form in the game you have a duty as a civilian to protect yourself and others from criminals. I've dealt with gangsters, killers and drug dealers my whole life. I can't be mad at some regular woman or man who works hard every day, pays their taxes and wants to live comfortably for wanting a drug dealer, killer, rapist or child molester to be caught even if it was my husband, brother or friend. Do you understand that? My mother was never in "the street game". She worked hard, paid taxes and bothered no one. She would be considered a witness to a crime; a civilian. Even if my mother had called the cops on me when she found drugs in my house years ago, I couldn't be mad at her. She was not in the game. The talk in the streets would have been *"Yo, Tee moms snitched on her."* When really my mother would have just been reporting a crime. I probably would have been mad, but I was a criminal. I was dealing drugs and that is illegal.

According to the streets, if you are in the game and you are considered a shooter or a gangster then you are expected to remain a stand-up guy by "street standards". Knowing you have a few bodies under your own belt the last thing people would expect of you is to be answering any questions that may be asked of you by any officer of the law.

This is where I draw the line on that "No Snitching" phrase. If you saw one of these disgusting men raping or molesting a child, you mean to tell me you're not going to say anything? Then you're a very ignorant individual. You have nothing to lose by putting these fools away knowing that they could have raped or molested a child.

You may not agree with me until it's your family or child that is killed or raped. Don't get me wrong, some of us still believe in street justice and I'm one of them. I'm just saying the justice system doesn't always work. When I mention street justice, I DO NOT mean killing another black man over something ignorant. I was expressing my feelings towards sex offenders. Again, I am not promoting violence, it's just my feelings towards these sick individuals.

Oh! I have another one. An incident happened to a hustler that I know, and a report was made. Next thing I know he's being called a snitch by of course someone he doesn't get along with. This guy was with his children and was robbed at gunpoint. Witnesses called the cops and when they came, he made the report. He is not a snitch. What is wrong with you all out here in these streets? Some of y'all have just taken this term and use it for any and every situation you could possibly use it for. It's wrong and it's disrespectful to label someone who was a victim of a crime.

According to some codes that no one has ever seen; When one is in the street game, the only expectation the streets have is that you remain **Honorable**. Everyone knows the consequences for their actions. There will always be risks and you're expected to take the good, which is getting lots of money, with the bad, which is a strong possibility of going to prison or even getting killed. Again, who made up the rules.

Now for my gangster dudes, killers and hustlers who are out there robbing and bullying people, I wasn't talking to you. You can't be shooters and then when a dude pulls up on you and tries to take your life, sit up in a precinct and be talking. It doesn't work that way. Right? Either you're about that life or you're not. There is no in between. The incident that I mentioned above was about a guy who hustled in the past. He's never been a bully. He's never been a loud mouth running around the town intimidating others. He was a father out with his children and minding his business.

**NOTE FROM MS TEE**: All hustlers ain't gangsters and all gangsters ain't hustlers. Every dude that's out in the street hustling is not a killer. Some have never killed anyone. If you carry yourself a certain type of way, killing is a very unnecessary act that can bring unwanted heat from the law. All gangsters ain't hustlers, which is why they are the one's killing others. They don't really know how to make money, so they have to kill, then take, then spend and start the cycle over again. Shall I refer back to a lack of education.

# $ THE GAME $

IT'S CRAZY HOW life sometimes throws us a curve ball that we never saw coming. One curve ball in the Urban Community was *"The Drug Game"* itself, *"The Fast life" "Hustling"*. Listen, none of us really knew what it was going to be like until we were in it. We all knew what the rewards could be by looking at those that experienced the drug game before us. If you chose to get in it, then you chose whatever came with it at that very moment. Some of us didn't care about the consequences. All we saw was green (money). Greed was the motivator.

No one was forced to enter the drug game. Everyone in the hood had the freedom to get in, and to get out. The money, the women and the risk are always enticing. Being looked up to as the "*tough guy*" or "*that guy*" is a feeling that most men want to experience especially if you're in the street life. Everyone wants to feel important, but we all know what we are and aren't built for. Then again sometimes we ourselves don't know how strong or weak we really are until that time comes when we are faced with making such challenging decisions.

I came up in the eighties and nineties when the streets of Harlem were overflowing with men and women in the game. It was such a happy time for me because it just seemed like everyone was having fun and enjoying life at the same time. I'm not saying that selling drugs and destroying our community was fun. At that same time, there was a sense of community. It was still a time when you respected your elders and your neighbor can whip you if you were caught doing something wrong. The streets were fun to be in and money was out there to be made. Everybody played their position and empires were being built. The people in the streets weren't doing anything new. They were just following behind those that came before them, perfecting their craft and putting their own little spin on things.

Although there were some female bosses in the game, men dominated it. I would be remiss if I didn't say it again that if it weren't for some women the men would not have been who they were. For the men that were making money, it was all about being "The Man". You get the money, then the cars and then you were guaranteed to get the women. That's it. That's what it was all about. With all that came the power and respect as well as unwanted hate and jealousy.

Everybody wanted a taste of the fast life. Unfortunately, some weren't ready for the risk that came with it. The risk was death or prison. Consider prison the better of the two. Think about it; you can still see your family, fight your case or just think about the changes you can make to your life that best fits you and your family when you are released (if parole is ever an option).

There are 3 decisions one may be expected to make when entering "The Game".

1. **BE A STAND-UP INDIVIDUAL AND STAND YOUR GROUND NO MATTER WHAT.**
2. **COMPROMISE YOUR INTEGRITY, LOYALTY AND RESPECT aka become an INFORMANT.**
3. **There is no 3...... Or Is there?**

But what if this happens. ***Hypothetically.***

3. Let's say that you were put in a position where there were no choices- i.e family members are threatened with jail time, yet they have not reaped any of the benefits from your drug dealings nor did they condone it. They wanted nothing to do with it. We all know how the FEDS get down. They will lie at times to get their man. They threaten to lock up mothers, grandmothers and take children away who had nothing to do

with your activities just to get you to snitch on others. What do you do?

Think about that third choice, especially when the government is playing dirty. I say it all the time the Government and the IRS are the real gangsters out here. They do what they want, when they want and guess what? Nine times out of ten we can't do nothing about it. Not too many went up against the government and won. Salute to those soldiers who chose to fight. I'm in no way giving anyone an out by mentioning that third option. It's just a realization that happens often.

So, what does one do? Do you challenge the system? Do you call the bluff of those savage cops that threaten your children, mother and grandmother? Sometimes they have absolutely no evidence, it's all circumstantial and they need you to fill in the blanks. This is the game that the government plays. It's not a game out here. Today in 2019 you must make some choices about what you want to do with your life. If you get caught up do you want to be the one to put a period at the end of that sentence. What sentence you ask? A sentence like this one:

> **COPS:** *"Who killed Andre Miller back in December over on Hill Side Avenue?"*
>
> **YOU:** *"Well I had nothing to do with it. All I know is that I heard Smoky from the south side saying he did it because he owed him some money.*
>
> **COPS:** *"Sit tight."*
>
> **You:** *"So are y'all gonna let me go now?"*

Although you didn't write a statement, you just filled in the blanks and became the period at the end of the sentence. You got picked up for a few bags of weed. That's peanuts compared to what Smoky is about to go through. It took you less than 10 minutes to change the life of a man whose hand you shook, broke bread with from time to time and sometimes called a friend. You just became a SNITCH!

The game sure ain't what some of us thought it was. I knew this book would pique the interest of quite a few of you. My question is which one are you? Are you *"A Standup Guy"* or *"A Snitch"*? Maybe you considered it doing what you had to do. Can you take full responsibility for your own actions or can you be persuaded by the government? Maybe you're just doing what you need to do to save your family. This is why I say today is the day you make a decision about doing right with your life or continuing to do wrong and ending up in a small room with a pad and pen in front of you with only 10 minutes to make a decision. Sometimes I laugh because I'm like "motherfucker it's only a no license stop. Calm down. You're not going to jail for life." Some of you men be ready to tell where the bodies at for a traffic stop. There's absolutely no need to be snitching for a red-light ticket. SMH!

By the way, are you asking yourself, why the hell would she write a book about snitching? Why not? Snitching has become a topic that everyone seems to be concerning themselves with. Someone said snitching is becoming out of control. No, it's been happening. I simply wrote this book because I'm tired of hearing a lot of misinformed dummies calling people snitches yet they have no idea about how many cooperators there really are walking these streets.

Have any of you ever been arrested and wondered how you slipped up because the cops got to you. For some reason you could not figure out how they found out what you were doing. For some reason the cops were able to raid your spot on the right day and at the right time. Was it just luck for the cops? No fool!! Somebody told on your ass that's how you got busted. You didn't slip up. You did everything except let the wrong person know what you were doing.

Since you couldn't figure it out you either took a plea deal or went to trial. The person that told never needed to take the stand because the lead they gave the police was good enough to get an indictment. There's no paper work floating around because it wasn't necessary. But it doesn't mean no one snitched on you. **THINK ABOUT IT!!**

# MR. UNTOUCHABLE

WHEN IT COMES to hustling, the rising and falling of empires in Harlem in the 70's and 80's, one name comes to mind... Yep. Mr. Untouchable aka Nicky Barnes. His name will always be synonymous with snitching, putting Guy Fisher away for life and taking down his crew. He took snitching to a level that was unbelievable. If you haven't seen that documentary you're in for a treat. It will blow you away. Pussy is allegedly why he lost his Goddamn mind. Pussy that belonged to his wife and mistress. He couldn't see it, feel it or smell it again. Allegedly his friends began messing around with the two women that he loved the most. He was doing FED time and he felt that his crew forgot about him. He became one of the most popular snitches of all time. Like I told you before, pussy is powerful and more potent than any drug on the streets. Well some pussy; I can't give all women credit for having good pussy. It's just a fact. (Lol) Sorry, now back to Nicky Barnes who chose to send quite a few men and women, which included his wife to prison. It was said that one of his friends was seen kissing his mistress Shamecka and his wife was seen in a car with one of his comrades while he was in prison. In his documentary there was a quote.

**"IF AN INJURY HAS TO BE DONE TO**

**A MAN**

**IT SHOULD BE SO SEVERE THAT**

**HIS VENGEANCE**

**NEED NOT BE FEARED."**

GODDAMN!!! That's some deep shit right there. Let that marinate. Do you need two more minutes to read that again? I'll wait. Now read it again if you must. I can't tell you how many times I read that quote over and over. My understanding of it is that if you want to do harm to the toughest and most feared person out there, your intentions would be to hurt them so bad that his comeback is not feared or even considered. Wow!! Nicky was a bad motherfucker. Relentless.

Believe it or not he wasn't the only one to do it. He wasn't the first to snitch and obviously wasn't the last. You had "official" mobsters and mob bosses turn into informants back in the late 70's and 80's. Joseph "The Ear" Massino was the boss of the Bonanno crime family. He made history as the first official Mob Boss to turn state's evidence. Who can forget "Sammy The Bull"? He was one of the most ruthless killers out there. And the list goes on? We all saw the movie "*American Gangster*". Frank Lucas did the 1-2 step.

Now Back to Nicky Barnes, a name that will always be attached to the gangster life in Harlem. This guy did what he did with no regrets and no remorse. After being incarcerated for a few years and feeling disrespected by his own crew aka "**The Council**" he set out to crush the empire he built, and he did it with a vengeance. Now if you don't mind being called a snitch, this is how you do it. I'm just saying. After so many years of having time to think about what he did, there was still no remorse from Mr. Untouchable. Hence, he ended up in the witness protection program. Let's not forget that.

I guess these days are no different from the old days. Why get angry over snitching? What's the point? It's never going to stop. The government has created a way to allow those who want another chance to go free at some point. They have created a way for one to beat the other to the punch. Hey, this could be you one day. Right? Would you not want the option? OR How about just staying legal so that this never has to be an option for you?

We really don't think of the consequences nor did we ever sit and think of what split decisions we would have to make in that small room knowing that there was a possibility that we could end up with a lot of time in prison.

Honestly none of us really know what we are capable of until shit hits the fan. But if you made the decision to participate in anything illegal that could possibly get you time in prison and you get caught, remember this is what you signed up for.

Nowadays some of you are telling before you get to the station without even realizing what you're up against. What the hell is wrong with you? Just asking. No judgement over here. Snitching has become the norm. Guess What? The view from the legal side of the world these days ain't bad. **THINK ABOUT IT!!**

# CHECK THE SCENARIO

ANYBODY CAN BE snitched on. I told a story once about how in 1989 I was riding uptown to take my boyfriends' grandmother something to eat when I heard shots. Instead of running to see what happened, I ran the food upstairs first then came back downstairs. Me and my friends rode over to 154th street and 8th Avenue and saw that some guy had been shot and killed. On our way back to my rental car two detectives stopped me saying-

> *"Excuse me miss, someone said that the victim was with you." I was like "y'all can't be serious."* –

Let's stop right there. **The cops were following me because they were investigating my boyfriend at the time. That murder was just a matter of convenience for them. It gave them the perfect opportunity to question me about my man at the time.** ----

So, what if someone really did say that the victim was with me. In 1989 there were no cameras like it is today. It would have been easy to say there's a camera on that store over there. I'm sure I would have gotten out of that situation, but damn how long would it have taken for me to prove myself just because someone said he was with me. Knowing who my man was at the time would not have made things any easier for me either.

Here are a few scenarios that has happened numerous times and unfortunately, it will continue. You decide what decision you would have made if it were you.

## SCENARIO 1:

Tone and his man Craig have been hustling and making money together for years. They came up as kids together. Tone was the dude that no matter what, made sure everybody ate. He was the one that would fight and protect the crew at all cost. Tone was the smart guy. Tone and Craig both have put in some work, laid a few dudes down and know each other's secrets. Craig gets knocked carrying 3 kilos of coke. This is his third felony and he's looking at an asshole full of time. Tone is still on the street, calling up lawyers and making sure Craig's family is doing good until he's back on the street. In the meantime, Craig has been booked and he's feeling the pressure. The police are visiting him every chance they get while waiting for him to be arraigned, but he has yet to tell Tone. And why? That's because Craig has already been thinking of a way to get out of this jam that can land him in jail for 25 years at least. Is Craig really going to do this to his man who held him down from the beginning and protected him in the streets from beef on many occasions.

Tone has much more to lose. He's been in the streets longer and he's the boss. You see Craig been slipping and this is his third felony. The money is really coming in right now and Tone is the man in the streets. Those boys would love to get dirt on him, but they can't. Tone's name has been ringing bells for a long time, but they haven't been able to get him because he's been smart, he's been careful, and he stays out the way. Now here comes Craig who knows all of Tone's business. He knows where the bodies are at. He knows the connect. He knows where the stash is and Tone's life as he knew it is about to come to a screeching halt all because Craig wasn't careful. (**Remember they came up as kids together.**)

Craig has decided to cooperate for less time in exchange for Tone's freedom. He has decided to use everything he knows about Tone against him. The statement has been written and signed and now he's being placed in protective custody. Craig just became a ***SNITCH***. He's the one who made the mistake. He slipped up and wasn't careful, but now Tone is about to pay for it....

**NOTE**: Craig didn't wait a cool 48 hours before running his mouth. The lawyer hasn't had a chance to make it to the arraignment. Although this is not his first bid, Craig wasn't really built for this. Who would have known? Especially since he's done a lot of dirt his damn self. He's even done a few short bids so this isn't his first time at the rodeo.

Where is the loyalty? When you are in business and whether it's legal or not, we usually deal with our best friends we grew up with or someone who we deem to be loyal enough to hold it down when things get rough. This is what the streets have come to. There is no honor amongst thieves. Has there ever been any honor?

What can Tone do now? Should Tone call Craig's bluff and force him to take the stand? Should he wait it out and let the investigation take its course? Does doing that give the cops enough time to find more snitches to make this case more concrete? Should Tone take a plea? Is telling on Craig an option? What do you think? This is the dilemma that many are forced to deal with.

This is how I see things; Whether a person is your best friend or not, but you know he's a real dude that will take care of business for you- snitching should never be an option. If I know Tone is my man and I know he will always be there for me and my family, I'm standing tall and fighting this until the end. More importantly it was my mistake. If I lose the case, I know that Tone will hold me and my family down. **NEVER** let the main nigga go down. **NEVER** let the money go down. Remember this was your mistake. Tone is the money. Tone has the ways and means to make things happen. Tone is the smart dude that must remain on the streets to make sure things get done. Tone will be so glad that you didn't tell on him (**although he should never have to think that you would**) that he's going to do everything in his power to get you out. He will make sure the lawyer gets you out or gets you the best deal possible. Craig is not thinking. If Tone gets knocked, who's going to look out for them and their families. Tone aka the money should be protected at all cost. Does that make sense? Some of you dudes out here are not thinking. **AGAIN, ARE YOU BUILT FOR THIS?**

## SCENARIO 2:

**January of 20??** A dude that's into bustin' checks and credit cards gets busted in Brooklyn. He's in the 79th precinct in Brooklyn and before he can hit the chair he says, "Hey, I know about a murder from 1992." The cops look at him as if they are interested in what he has to say. This guy proceeds to tell them about the murder. He tells who was there, when it happened and mentions the guns that were used. This dude just became a **SNITCH.** One of the officers happened to know one of the names that was mentioned and calls the girlfriend of one of the alleged suspects. Her man is already out of town in prison doing time for another charge and is scheduled to be released in 6 months. The cop met with homie's girl and tells her what's going on. She nods her head as she listens. She's very familiar with the story and knows that whoever is sitting in that precinct is a definite threat. She's sure of it because she was there when the murder occurred many years ago.

Now the cop says to the chick- *"So what do you want me to do?"* She offers up an explanation- "My man didn't do it. John did it." Now his girl is from the street and knows the game hands down. This was an easy one for her. "John is dead at this time so a little snitching can't hurt the dead. The cop goes on to say "okay, John did it, case closed. The chick asks the cop-

*"By the way what's homies name that's in there talking?"*

The detective smiles and says-

*"Come on Tee I can't tell you that."* They both smile and walk their separate ways.

He knew better because it's possible the guy would have been found with his tongue stuck in his ass somewhere. I'm just saying.

- My problem with this story is that the guy got picked up for credit cards that may have carried

a sentence of a year or 2. Yet he's willing to give up 3 dudes and put them away for 25 years or 5 to 15 on a plea. What's happening here?

Although it helps their cases at times, some cops really don't respect snitches. Look how this coward was so willing to go decades back to dig up a body.

For the record this scenario is **NOT FAKE**. It's true. Thank GOD this cop remembered the girl from all those years ago. Personally, I like having cops as friends. Fuck that. Cops respect real people trust me when I tell you. They will protect you too. Trust me I know.

Back to this guy here. What if her man was approached by some other cop with all the information and told him about the witness that was willing to testify? There's a possibility that he would not have wanted to take a chance and blow trial. This means he would have taken a plea to do 5 to 15 that would hopefully had run concurrently. Don't forget her man was already in prison down south for an assault. Now the snitch would have either gotten off altogether or did six months for credit card and check schemes all because he wasn't built for it.

What if the cop didn't know the female? This guy never wrote a statement, nor would he have had to testify because her man would have taken a plea most likely. The dude is still a SNITCH. My point is, **ALL SNITCHES DON'T HAVE A PAPER TRAIL.** Steering the cops in one's direction is still snitching. So, stop yelling all that **"WHERE'S MY/THE PAPER WORK BULLSHIT"**. You know what you did. A lot of you know what you've done. I'm just saying.

\*\*\*\*\*\*\*\*\*\*\*\*\*\*\*\*\*\*\*\*\*\*\*\*\*\*\*\*\*\*\*\*\*\*\*

Me and a friend of mine was having a conversation about the streets and this subject in particular. He said, *"Tee what niggas don't know is that if you and your man get caught up and one of them take a plea, they just indirectly snitched on their man."* I was like

*"DAMN!!! You are right".* He said, *"When they take that plea, they are admitting guilt."* What do you think?

## SCENARIO 3:

AJ and King get caught in a rental car with a trunk full of cocaine. There are about 10 kilos of coke hidden under the spare tire canal. There may be a way of getting out of this one though. While AJ and King are being booked, AJ assures King that they can get out of this jam.

1. **The car is a rental**
2. **There is no proof that it belongs to them**
3. **With the help of the lawyer that he is going to pay for they'll be out soon**

King is nervous. You can see **"We"** are guilty all over his face. AJ knows he's the stronger out of the two, but he keeps assuring King that they will be okay. AJ has the money needed to pay the lawyer to make sure this case never sees a jury, but it may take a while.

At the first arraignment they plead not guilty. King is given a high cash bail, but AJ is held for a warrant on a minor marijuana charge as well as a parole violation. AJ instructs his people to get King out. Again, he's letting King know that he got his back. The next court date is in 35 days. In the meantime, King was contacted by the prosecutor, who stated that because he has priors and the seriousness of this case it is not looking good for them, so he needs to think about himself at this point. In King's mind he is in a dilemma. The lawyer has been in contact with him as well. The lawyer told King not to worry because AJ is paying all the costs and the case is bullshit. "There's no way he can't beat these charges."

Now what do you think King should do? Should he ride with his man AJ and hold out? 10 Kilos of cocaine is a lot. But the lawyer they have is one of the best. As the court date approaches AJ and King have spoken on the phone and all seemed well.

On the next court date, the court officers bring AJ out from the back. King gets up and joins AJ and the lawyer to face the judge, but then some short white court appointed lawyer comes flying into the court room apologizing for being late. AJ and the lawyer look at each other curious as to who she is while King never batted an eye and continued to look forward. AJ's lawyer is preparing for hearings as well as asking for a dismissal for an illegal search. The short white attorney interrupts introducing herself as King's new attorney and informs the court that her client wants to change his plea. AJ and his lawyer look over at King like "FOR REAL MOTHERFUCKER". King continues to look forward not batting an eye. She continues with *"My client would like to change his plea to guilty."* BOOM!!!!! **KING JUST ADMITTED GUILT AND ESSENTIALLY SNITCHED ON AJ.!!**

Does the prosecutor plan on using King to snitch on AJ? What are your thoughts?

**Please note that there is a possibility that AJ can still beat the charges.**

Before talking with my friend, I hadn't even thought about a scenario like this although it's very common. When my friend brought this up my mouth was opened, like wow. He was right. If you and someone get caught up together and one wants to fight, but the other pleads guilty, this can be used to indict and convict.

I'm sure someone reading this has made this move or they're thinking about it. If so, you may be considered a snitch. No judgement here. **THINK ABOUT IT!!**

# NOTHING WRONG WITH BEING LEGAL

I N MY FIRST book I told a story about a friend of mine who was hustling in the streets for a while but ended up going legal. This guy got a job and he felt good about it. He said *"Tee, it feels so good to be working. I'm not stressed. I'm not looking over my shoulder at night. I'm happy."* He said, *"It feels so good to get a check."* I was so proud of him because it showed growth.

Now going back to the scenarios, you just read-Would you rather end up in these situations or would you rather be legal? You are now being educated about how it goes down. You got the blueprint in your hands of how your life can end up if you keep hustling, gang banging etc. Your name could possibly replace those fictitious names you just read about. Although I have more to share with you in a few, this should be enough for you to make an adult decision regarding your future.

Stop listening to some of these so-called hustlers and gangsters in the streets talking about snitches, not snitching, standing tall and "keeping it real". Guess who won't be sending you any money when you're locked up? Guess who won't be making sure your wife and kids are eating? Guess who won't be concerned about the rent and the light bill being paid? Guess who won't be keeping it real when you're rotting away in prison? Yep, those same dudes who was giving you that bad advice. Why allow "the streets" to dictate what you do, how you move as well as the future for you and your family?

This is the time to be smart. This is the time for growth. This is the time to ask yourself is it worth it. This is the time to be real with oneself and ask-Am I ready for the consequences? Do I want to walk around being labeled? Do I want to keep it real and take 25 years of my life rotting away in prison?

For those of you that are still in the streets, these are the questions that you should be asking yourself. For those of you in prison, soon to be released, these are the questions you should not want to ever ask yourselves again.

Only a sucker who knows better would question whether being legal is better than being in the streets. Only a sucker would allow the streets to tell them that a job is for suckers.

Anybody who lives in NY has the upper hand at being an entrepreneur. Unless you travel to China, we have the best, wholesale district out here. So, if you don't like working a 9 to 5 or having a boss, become an entrepreneur.

Again, this is the blueprint that can change your life. You can stop hustling right now and choose your family over the streets. Don't let an uneducated gangster be the reason you made a dumb decision.

# RULES

LET'S TALK ABOUT the rules of the game. Are there any rules? Who made up the rules? Are all bets off when it comes to the game? In the game we say what we think people should do. We expect for individuals to act accordingly, but according to what? Why isn't it right to beat one to the punch of freedom before he beats you to it?

Let's talk Alpo and Wayne Perry for a minute. Wayne Perry was an individual that in my mind could be categorized as a Psychopath. He was allegedly one of the most dangerous men in his town. He allegedly killed for fun. He allegedly killed men and women for fun and possibly children. Where we come from in the Urban community most dudes in the game was killed fighting over territory, drugs, women and money. I am not saying that it was right, but it's the truth. It's said that Wayne Perry showed no remorse for any of the murders that he committed until he was locked up. I assume he never put any thought into what he was doing or why he was doing it. In my opinion the only reason guys in D.C are mad at Alpo is because he is from N.Y. He came to their town and made hundreds of thousands of dollars. He engaged people and got them to trust him. He strategically put a plan together by bailing Wayne out when no one else would. Alpo was able to engage and get the strongest and most feared guy from D.C to hold him down, help him make hundreds of thousands of dollars. AND THEN! Alpo was the one that put him away for life.

I'm sure, there were a whole lot of D.C. residents that were glad that Wayne Perry was off the streets. I know this because I spoke to a few. But for the fact that Alpo was able to come to your town, get into Wayne's good graces and get money, then turned around and was the one who put him away is the only reason they hate him. It's funny because when Wayne's bail was ten thousand dollars no one in D.C. bailed him out. I wonder why? Was it because you guys didn't want him back on the streets in fear of eventually becoming his next victim?

I guess Alpo didn't play by these so-called rules huh. Why is Harlem so mad? Is it because he killed someone you all adored even though you've never even met the victim? Unfortunately, we must charge those casualties to the game.

So, what's up with those rules. Are there any rules to the game? Or Are we supposed to assume that there are rules and live our lives for the streets that don't, hasn't ever and will never love us back?

I had a conversation with an individual that cooperated, and he said-

> "Tee, the streets don't care about nobody. The streets are always talking about keeping it real. If I had kept it real, I would be doing life and possibly had the death penalty." He

said *"I saw for myself how the streets turn their backs on people. I saw dudes pressing the red button when their friends and people they owed money to would call."*

I thought about that because I've seen it many times myself. Dudes will go to prison and their friends and even family would go on with their lives and forget all about them. A letter can go a long way for someone who is rotting away in prison. I have been able to keep good friendly relationships with a lot of real men. I know what getting a letter means to people that are away. Sometimes they need that escape. So just engaging one with a letter and answering a call occasionally means a lot.

So, what are the Rules of Engagement when a fellow soldier goes in and stand up the way the "streets" want them to? Why aren't you engaging them? Why aren't you keeping it real with them? This may be a reason, not an excuse, that guys do what they do. No one is keeping it real when their so-called friends get behind those walls.

Another interesting thing this guy said was-

*"Tee, where is the keeping it real trust fund."*

I didn't have an answer for that, but it sure made me think. When your friends and others go to prison and do either long stints or even life in prison, who is in charge for making sure they eat, get letters and have all the things they need to survive in the system? Who looks out for their families? Who makes sure their children and wives are eating and bills are paid? Who does the hospital visits to their parents who might be aging? Who has engaged themselves in these situations? I'm waiting for an answer. Do you think you're obligated to do so?

Some dudes are sitting in prison not because they wanted to; Not because they were stand up men; Not because snitching never entered their minds. It's because they wanted to keep it real for the streets who turned around and didn't keep it real with them.

When we talk about the so-called rules and codes of the streets, what are the incentives for doing what the streets expect you to do. **THINK ABOUT IT!!!!!!!**

If someone can send me a copy of these rules and codes, I would deeply appreciate it. My address is in the back of this book. I've been in the streets for a long time and I haven't come across a copy or the author yet.

# ALPO

I WASN'T GOING TO mention "Alpo" again in this book, but I must. Plus, after that surprising call to the podcast back in February I had to come back and insert some things. Some of you might get mad or you might respect what I'm saying. Either way it is what it is.

We all know the Rich Porter and Wayne Perry stories, so I don't need to go into it again. Actually, I don't understand the fascination with the two, but hey I'm not hating. After meeting Albert my views about his character and him as a person had changed. He wasn't arrogant or full of himself. He was very respectful, charismatic and had a personality that was very inviting. I've grown to admire this guy's bravery, his guts and the fact that he lives his life for himself and not according to what others think. I've spoken to quite a few people who know him, and everybody said the same thing- *"That's a cool guy." "I like him." "He's just living his life."* It's not that he's walking around like superman or bragging about what he did, not at all. I asked him how it feels to be out and how does it feel to be called a snitch. He said:

*Ms. Tee, Yes, I told, and yet I still did 24 years in prison. I didn't tell and walked out a free man. I did time for my crimes as well. I did Twenty-four years in prison. I dodged the death penalty and now I just want to live my life. I have no problem wearing the "Snitch" hat if they want me too. There are many who I allowed to remain unbothered by the law who was in the game and did business with me. They live in Harlem, DC and Virginia. I could have brought them all down, but I didn't. I had love for these people and decided to keep them safe. The ones from NY are from the music industry. They are still very influential in the industry today. So, to them I want to say, you're welcome. Right now, I have enough people that love and care for me to be okay with the decision I made. I did what I needed to do for my family. I understand the views of those that do not agree with what I did, but I have no regrets. I hear what people say and it's cool to an extent. Now although I did what I did, I am still a man and being soft or weak is not one of my attributes.* -- **ALPO**

Let me tell you why I respect this guy. Unlike a lot of precinct snitches talking about they're not on paper, I can respect his honesty, which does not mean I agree or disagree with what he did. What he did does not affect me or you. He did what he did with no regrets. He walks in his truth everyday wearing a label that most men won't admit to. He's hated for killing someone that a lot of people admired, although more than half of you never even met Rich. He snitched on a dude and put him away for life and never once did he deny it or make an excuse for what he's done. Unlike others, he told the truth about what he did and why he did it. His reason was that he did what he needed to do to survive. Albert said he does not promote snitching nor would he ever glorify it, he just needed to do what was best for him. That's it. Plain and simple.

Please don't misconstrue my words. I'm not saying that I have respect for people that cooperate. I just don't care anymore. I do respect the fact that unlike some other men, Albert admitted to what he did, he walks in his truth and the opinions of the streets don't matter to him. He was not going to "Keep it Real" for the streets.

I will say this; he may be the first one that has done what he's done and refuses to allow "the streets" to dictate his life and how he moves.

Everyone knows what Albert has done. There is no guessing or suspicions. He's told his story and he wears his truth whether we respect what he's done or not.

Like I mentioned a few chapters back, there are a lot of informants walking around. We speak to them. We eat and drink with them. We are discussing private business with them. I'm around a lot of you who suspect certain dudes that may not be "right", but you still speak to them and deal with them in some manner. Don't be surprised if they are sitting back collecting data so that when they are picked up again, they are equipped to railroad you. I'm just saying. Never will they admit it. Never will they want to wear the "snitch hat". They are just hiding in plain sight.

# ANONYMOUS

**THIS GENTLEMAN HERE has been down for a long time now. He and I discussed what's going on in the streets these days. This is how he feels about snitching in his words:**

I was affected by that shit.....I did 263 months in the feds over niggahs telling on me....I couldn't believe it...stone cold killers... I went to trial and these niggahs got on the stand and pointed me out.... If it wasn't for Obama, I would still be in the feds doing 480 months... I wouldn't of came over to Ohio until I was 60 years old. That snitching shit is pure weakness.......I know rats that bust their guns in prison...ain't going for shit...I ain't either...so I was wiling to paint the wall red getting at rats...nowadays it's out of hand and it ain't no winning in that chasing them down shit..... I stay in my lane....I hate it when niggahs talk that gangster shit....and it comes out they told...smh... I know about Kev Chiles story...it was talked about.....I know about Tom Cross too... I can never do business with a person like Po because of what he stood for... you can never correct what he did...that's something that he got to deal and live with.....Kev....I can make moves with him but I know that he is weak.. He just doesn't have the heart to spill blood or whatever....but both of them are different types of cowards....there is a word for them...it's "recreant"...it means cry for mercy or yielding in a cowardly manner ...unfaithful to duty or allegiance.....a cowardly wretch... one who forsakes a duty....a cause...one that is unfaithful...I just stay in my lane Ma....I'm in here for a murder I did not do or know anything about....I was offered immunity back in 1996 but refused.....I think about all the other shit I did and got away with....and how many is in the dirt ....and how many maybe were wrongfully convicted over something I did.....you get back what you put in the universe......I'm in here for some shit I don't know about...but I will never trade someone else's life in to this shit for my freedom...I know that I'll give all this shit back....I may cannot make up for the lost time...but I can look myself in the mirror...or move around like I want to...knowing I am morally correct ....

I know Kev and Po may feel how they went about their situations was the best for them...they got to live with that..... but I will talk to Kev....and never talk to Po..... I can never glorify or invite the younger generation to live like this.....selling drugs.. killing... destroying communities and brag about it. or feed illusions to people like shit is ok.....that's why these kids is in the game...getting caught...and telling like crazy now...My ole head told me about his campaign he's doing called "From the school yard to the prison yard to graveyard" he pushes worldwide....you can't make the younger kids stay away.. but you can warn them and enlighten them of the consequences..... Dude is my ole head...I known him since the 80's..... I was groomed by older cats....was walked through to know what to do and not do....

I remember that niggah Vance from your way in Harlem....that niggah was hiding who he was and what case he was on and where he was from......telling cats he was from Delaware... but had family in NY.....I use to eat and break bread with Vance...he was calling himself "Veto"..... Unique got there and didn't tell us shit...he knew son was swine.... I left them in Cali in 02... Fat Leon came to Lee county....I told him that I couldn't stop the decision that he couldn't live on that compound...we were in Terre Haute together.. I didn't know he was swine too...A dude from Harlem kept it a secret cause they were squeezing him....Leon let me read his whole case.. I read everything...that's how I found out about Veto being Vance.... I caught up to him and let cats get at him.... niggahs did him dirty.... he lucky I ain't stab him....he got cut real bad....and stomped out viciously ( he told on that too)... he is now hiding in the Muslim community ...with a big beard.. I stay in my lane...I'm too old for that now...chasing these rats....the game is FUCKED UP!!!!

Anyway Tee....I just wrote K yesterday..... I need you to blow.....real heads need to be in control...people can learn from your stories.. we need someone to talk and relate to these young (and old too) black/Hispanic females (sisters).... you can be that voice....

Anyway....tell me where to send your paper for my copy.... I better get an autographed special edition version too... SMILE..

**This was sent to me by someone that is friends with me and a few dudes that I was involved with. These are all his words. I copied and pasted it. I deleted some things about certain people that didn't need to be in this book. Please note, I decided to make him anonymous. It doesn't matter who he is. How he feels is what's important.**

# PROFFER AGREEMENT

**P**ROFFER OR «QUEEN FOR a day» letters are written **agreements** between federal prosecutors and individuals under criminal investigation which permit these individuals to tell the government about their knowledge of crimes, with the supposed assurance that their words will not be used against them in any later proceedings.

I hope you understand what this means. If not, I'm going to go a little further and explain it. I'm about to shut all y'all uneducated individuals up. I'm tired of hearing people talk about who is or isn't a snitch. I'm tired of hearing y'all shout out "Stop Glorifying Rats". If the snitch didn't do anything to affect you, be thankful and keep it moving. If you are not or never was in the game, then why are you speaking on this subject.

This chapter here is very necessary for a whole lot of you out there running your mouths. I do understand that you are ignorant to the ways of how the government works. Therefore, class is in session. Also, after this I would love to hear your responses after you've eaten your words.

Along with the meaning above a **"Proffer Agreement"** also expects for an individual not only to tell about all the crimes they've done, the agreement is for them to tell **WHO** they did the crimes with and **WHO** if so, they did the crimes for. Did you hear me? So, this means they had to **COOPERATE** with the government in order to get a deal other than life in prison or the death penalty. This means that some of y'all big homies, brothers, ya' mans and em' and even some of y'all daddies had to give it up in order to get 25, 30, 35 and maybe even a 40-year prison term to avoid longer sentences and maybe even death.

I said all that to say, do your homework on EVERYBODY before you talk about ANYBODY. Just because someone does the time stated above does not mean they didn't cooperate on some level. Alpo signed one, but he was verbal and honest about it. Let's see if others are verbal and honest about what they did. Let's see if they will ever admit to what they agreed to. How about y'all ask some of these big homies if they signed a Proffer. Y'all heard about some of the gangsters in Harlem, Bronx, Queens and Brooklyn and what they did. Some of them don't have life. WHY? Mmmm hmmmm... Figure it out.

Listen I already said it; the government has afforded such opportunities for people who have committed crimes. There are all kinds of cooperators in these streets and about to come home. One cooperation DOES NOT trump the other. This means that there are a lot more "snitches" out here if you want to go there. A snitch is a snitch. Right? You can't pick and choose which snitch you want to deal with. If you deal with one, then you should deal with them all. If you are against snitches, then you are against them all.

I bet some of y'all are looking crazy right now and you should. You thought homie took that time like a champ huh? Nope. He cooperated in some way, shape or form.

Wayne Perry, although he may be kicking himself in the ass right now, took his like a real champ. Wayne was asked to just tell on himself for a deal and he refused to tell on himself about any other murders he may have done that could possibly be solved. I was told that he refused to do it because he also did not want to see Alpo tell on him. I heard Wayne said this " Judge give me my time so I can get out of here."

Wayne Perry received natural life. Now that's some stand up shit right there.

Again, there are more snitches in the streets than you know. Gully TV did an interview with a retired Federal Agent and she stated that 85% to 90% of the cases would not be solved without cooperation. Some of these gangsters that y'all look up to have signed a Proffer Agreement.

Educating myself about what a Proffer Agreement means is the reason why I changed my perspective on this subject. The government will keep offering and there are those that will keep accepting the offer. Stop fooling yourselves thinking some guys are above cooperating with the Federal Government. This just tells me that all of you who have concerned yourselves with "Snitching" need to find something else to concern yourselves with like getting a job, your GED, taking care of your kids and paying some child support. What you think? **THINK ABOUT IT!!!!**

# HARLEM PULL UP
# A CHAIR

P LEASE BE ADVISED that the statements I am about to make is for anyone who wants to listen. Right now, I am talking to Harlem because this is where I am from. There is a reason why this chapter came about. I am a female that quite a few people share information with. I know a lot that goes on in the streets. I get wind of private meetings and phone calls between certain people. I'm just that type of person that people trust. I'm not here to call out any names or embarrass anyone, but some of you are behaving as if you're unable to make your own decisions.

Let me start by saying that nobody in Harlem or from Harlem has ever had the authority to dictate what another individual can or should be doing. I heard and saw things that prompted me to talk about this. Everyone is entitled to make their own decisions as individuals. We will not always agree therefore we can agree to disagree; we can discuss our differences of opinions and whether we like it or not the end decisions of all parties should be respected.

This is for the men right now. It's embarrassing how I see and hear how some of you allow another individual to dictate how you move, who you associate with and how you think. Why are you afraid of what another man feels? Does he pay your bills? Does he take care of your children? Someone else's beliefs should not affect yours.

When it comes to snitching a lot of people feel it's wrong. There are people that I know who stand on being totally against it. They will never speak to nor have anything to do with a snitch. They want nothing to do with those individuals. Although they feel this way, it is not their mission to bother these individuals. They would rather just stay away and that is totally fine. I understand them.

Then you have people that are neutral. They don't care one way or the other. They too may think it's wrong, but they may greet the individual in passing and keep it moving. Their idea is that what was done didn't affect them so it's not their business.

Then you have people that have spoken to "the snitch" and after the conversation they take a liking to the individual. During the conversation their perspective of this individual changed a bit. But now the streets and their friends have heard about it and their story has changed. Why? Why are you scared or embarrassed that a known snitch has changed your opinion of them? It's okay. What's not okay is that you run around making excuses and changing stories because of someone else's opinion. As an adult we are all entitled to make our own decisions despite how the streets feel. **STOP** living for the streets that has never cared for you. The same people that you try to live for will be the ones that talk about you, use you and will hurt you. If they can't respect you and your adult decisions, then you should re-evaluate your relationships. Just something to think about.

Another thing I want to mention is that there are individuals, gangsters, hustlers etc. speaking out against snitches and condemning them. They are talking about street codes that we should be living by. What I learned is that they have friends that snitched. They still deal with them, yet they are telling others to stay away from snitches. They are hypocrites. So, does this mean they get to pick and choose which snitches they can deal with? They can do it, but everyone else can't. I'm sorry but it does not work that way. Either you're against it or not. They can't have it both ways. Be careful with who's trying to dictate what you should and shouldn't be doing. Some pick and choose which snitch they are cool with just because it's their friend. SMH! Either they like snitches or they don't.

To the naysayers this is for you who have never been in the drug game, street life and have never seen the inside of a jail cell. Why do you criticize others that you do not know? How can you have an opinion on a topic that you know nothing about? It amazes me to watch some of you criticizing, name call and yell out of line when you yourself don't know what you are capable of. You're a follower who can't think for yourselves. You are someone who goes along with what you think the streets want you to do. You are someone who just wants to fit in. You are someone who's scared to show your real self. You are scared to give your own opinion because you are afraid of what others would think about you. That's who you are. You're a coward.

One thing about me is that I will give my opinion and have a debate with you if it's something that I strongly believe in. I've never been one to go along with what others think or feel, just because. No, I am a leader with my own individual opinions that I can express without fear of what someone else thinks. What I will say is this: I refuse to let what others think dictate how I feel and what I do. As an adult I will make decisions according to my own beliefs. I will never fear someone else's judgement of me. I don't expect anyone to always agree with me, but I do expect you to respect my decisions as an individual.

The naysayers are always the ones who has yet to experience what someone else has been through. The naysayers always got an opinion. How about a solution sometimes? How about reaching out and having a decent and intelligent conversation with someone and formulating your own opinion.

**THINK ABOUT IT!!**

# PEPE LE PEW

S OME OF US that are of a certain age remember this cartoon character right here. He was a skunk that ran around looking for love and acceptance, but his odor kept him from finding it. Well I think this chapter speaks volumes for a funky dude from Harlem that was running around looking for acceptance. He didn't have an odor, but for many years he did have a black cloud of suspicions over him.

I first met him up in Fishkill Correctional Facility around 2010 while visiting my man at the time. This dude and my good friend Mike were friends as well. Mike really looked out for this guy. Mike made sure he had clothes, food and even took females to visit him. That's what a real dude is suppose to do for a "friend"; especially when they're in that type of situation. It makes there time on the inside a little better. (Refer back to chapter "RULES")

My man and this dude both got out around 2012. The dude did 27 years and my man did 24 years in prison. They both acclimated back to society rather quickly. My man really liked the dude. That was his man. The dude was also close to an O.G that I've known for over 30 years.

This dude started getting money and he opened a juice bar. He and my O.G ran the town partying and having a good time. The dude was all on the gram taking photos, so life looked like it was good for him. Now listen, even though things look good on the outside, there are times when temptations come into play especially when you need some extra cash. Those of us that are from the street know how needing extra cash can be. If opportunity presents itself temptation can come into play. If it looks good, we just might take the risk. We'll run and buy a few grams or ounces of something to sell to make a quick buck. That's all good as long as we all take responsibility for our own actions.

Now the tables turned in 2014 for my best friend Mike. He ended up in the FEDS and he needed this dude to send him a few dollars. He was in no way asking for the same favors that he had done for him. All he wanted was twenty-five dollars here, fifty dollars there. Short paper. The dude was rolling so how could he not look out for a real brother like Mike that was there for him at one point. He's got a juice bar and getting a few dollars so fifty dollars won't hurt his pockets at all. Right?

I saw the dude on 8th Avenue and pulled over one day to ask for some money to send to Mike and he tells me to call him Tuesday. I thought to myself, *"my nigga, call you Tuesday for fifty dollars"*. I had the money but being that I knew what Mike did for him, he needed to come up out his pockets with some money. I told Mike that this dude is going to give him the run around. And I meant give him the run around, not me because I'd be damned if I allowed anybody to have me chasing them for fifty dollars. Right then and there this skunk had me tight. He was a user and very unappreciative for what Mike did for him. He could not have known what the word friend meant at all.

Remember that black cloud of suspicions I spoke of earlier? For years rumors had already been swirling around the streets that this dude was a snitch from back in the day. Allegedly a dude broke his jaw on the inside some years back because of that rumor. Nobody could never confirm those accusations though. There was no paper work from my understanding but remember what I told you about paper work; sometimes there is no paper trail. The O.G and my man went at every one that called this dude a snitch. They protected his name with their lives. They loved this dude and cared about him that much. We all know how a rumor like that can destroy someone's reputation, but the O.G and my man were in for a hell of a surprise.

Let me tell you about a GREAT guy from Harlem named Wayne-O aka Bump. He and my man were like brothers. Wayne-o allegedly did his thing in the streets and was getting money. Now I personally don't know all the dealings that Wayne and this other dude had if any, but in 2015 the skunk made a decision that would change Bump's life and turn Harlem upside down.

Around October of 2015 the skunk allegedly gets caught with about 22 grams of heroin and gets a bail. Let me remind you that he was still on Parole from that 27-year bid. In the back of some people's mind they wondered how he got a bail, but hey things happen. Fast forward to March of 2016 the news and newspapers were filled with information on a huge drug bust that netted about 10 to 15 suspects and Wayne Green aka Wayne-O was one of them.

Yep, this dude snitched and got one of the most liked and well-respected dudes from Harlem locked up. Wayne and a few friends of mine were a part of that group of suspects that got caught up in that sting. They took all of Wayne's money, jewelry and took a good man from his elderly mother, wife and children.

I met Wayne thru my man and he always seemed like a good dude. I personally couldn't say that he was a good guy, but he must have been a great guy because when he got locked up, I've never seen the streets react the way they did. The streets were hurt to hear what happened to this guy. It was unbelievable. Men and women had tears in their eyes because:

1) **They knew it may be over for Wayne**
2) **He was a great dude that helped everyone**
3) **All because a snitch couldn't do time for the 22 grams that he allegedly chose to buy.**

My man and the O.G had to eat their words and literally apologize to all the people that they argued with, cursed out and even stopped dealing with because they were calling the dude a snitch from the beginning. Can you imagine how they felt?

This time the dude wasn't being called a snitch based off a coincidence or a rumor. Oh no, we saw the paperwork. Now you can see it. The paperwork says it all. I crossed out his government name because his son begged me too and I don't want to be responsible if someone tries to harm him. This is just to show you how things go down. But it's there in black and white and he couldn't deny it. Copies were made, and the streets were flooded with them. It was only right that this was done because of the move he made instead of standing up like a man and doing his time because he slipped up. He chose not to take responsibility for his own actions. The paperwork states that he gave the cops Wayne's phone number and any pertinent information that could be used to make an arrest.

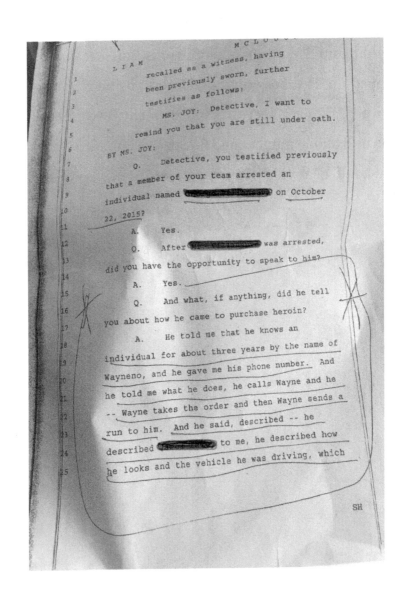

L I A M    M C L O U D

recalled as a witness, having been previously sworn, further testifies as follows:

MS. JOY: Detective, I want to remind you that you are still under oath.

BY MS. JOY:

Q.    Detective, you testified previously that a member of your team arrested an individual named ▆▆▆▆▆▆▆ on October 22, 2015?

A.    Yes.

Q.    After ▆▆▆▆▆▆ was arrested, did you have the opportunity to speak to him?

A.    Yes.

Q.    And what, if anything, did he tell you about how he came to purchase heroin?

A.    He told me that he knows an individual for about three years by the name of Wayneno, and he gave me his phone number. And he told me what he does, he calls Wayne and he -- Wayne takes the order and then Wayne sends a run to him. And he said, described -- he described ▆▆▆▆▆ to me, he described how he looks and the vehicle he was driving, which

SH

McLoughlin

was a blue Honda Odyssey. And during that conversation he said he gets $60 for a gram for heroin, gets $60 a gram.

Q.     Did he also indicate that he calls the individual that he knew as Wayne or Wayneno big brother?

A.     Yes.

MS. JOY:  I have no further questions for this witness. Any from the grand jurors?  Seeing none, you are excused.

THE WITNESS:  Thank you, again.

(WITNESS EXCUSED)

I couldn't believe it when I saw this dude in the gas station in 2017 on 233$^{rd}$ and Webster Avenue. He had snitched on a good guy from Harlem but was still lying about it. He was in his convertible BMW, top down and the music blasting like he didn't snitch on anyone and like his paperwork wasn't copied and spread throughout the streets of Harlem. I couldn't believe it. This guy snitched and put a few people away just because he got caught with 22 grams of heroin and didn't want to go back to jail. Yet he was acting as if he did nothing wrong. He had been out maybe 4 years after doing 27 years in prison, but at some point, he chose to get back in the game. No one forced him.

That dude could have done 2 to 3 years and I know for a fact that Wayne-O would have made sure he was good because that's the kind of man he was.

So, I would like to send a shout out to Wayne, Kirk, Rubin and the others that got caught up in that mess that dude made. He destroyed lives and households. I might sound a little bias compared to the other stories that I mention in this book, but this one was a very unnecessary situation as well as more personal to me because Mike is my longtime friend.

Somebody might be saying that I'm glorifying drug dealers and drug dealers should be in jail anyway. Yes, when the police catch them, but not because some dude can't do time for 22 grams.

For those of you that want to blame drug dealers and don't care who snitches on them, how about we start with the government, they started bringing drugs into our communities in the first place. They wanted to destroy us. Do your research and go back to the seventies and eighties to see how the drug epidemic began.

So, I hope his funky ass is somewhere finally realizing what he did was wrong because from what I hear he's still trying to deny it. He had already told my man he did it and tried to offer an explanation, but there was nothing he could say to justify his actions.

For the rest of you, take this as a lesson. Don't allow your names to be on some paperwork that floats throughout the streets and the jail system. If the streets are not for you and in your heart, you know that doing time is something that you will never be ready for; then re-evaluate how you move and do something different. I respect that more than anything.

**I did not put this paperwork in here to embarrass anyone, or to get anyone harmed. This is to show what happens and it is up to you to make a conscious decision if the game is for you or not.**

This one was for my friend Michael Crew. See you soon.

# PREACHER

I DIDN'T KNOW PREACHER personally. My uncle Stan was cool with him and his son. I met his son through Stan. Preacher became an informant and snitched on his crew and his family including his children. Preacher was a very dangerous man who was into kidnapping, extortion and dismembering people. Yep, he was the real deal.

One of my good friends who I speak to often was down with Preacher. He's still doing time right now. When preacher decided to turn, my friend was offered 27 years, but ended up with 35 years. At the time he was only around 27 years old himself. Let this marinate. Can you imagine being 27 and being sentenced to 35years? You can lose your mind in the court room hearing that. And my friend did. He went bananas. I asked my friend what happened back then. He sent me an email telling me what Preacher said to him:

*"His famous last words 2 me was :"Look no further than them bathrooms son I brought you in here" Meaning he "snitched on me" 2 get me in the Fed System... (Smhs). My last famous words 2 him was "You been running from the police all ya life 2 end up running 2 them NOW 2 get their help!!! (Smhs)... it fucked him up Tee he was literally stuck 4 words 2 come back at me with!!! ... I used that "Old School Wisdom on him from back when he was growing up wit my Uncle's & them..."*

Isn't that crazy what Preacher said to him. Can you imagine someone telling you that? Someone you were loyal too. Preacher was a very manipulative individual who had people putting in major work for him and he betrayed them all. Look at how one of the most feared men in Harlem could turn around and tell on his whole crew. Preacher even snitched on his kids. What happened to those rules? They were nowhere to be found. No one was safe from his wrath.

Preacher is locked up now for life and he's in population. If anyone steps to him, they better step right. From what I hear, he's still about that life even in there. He has nothing to lose and he has nothing but time to get up in somebody's ass in more ways than one at that. If you from Harlem, you know what I'm talking about.

For the record, everybody in Harlem wasn't scared of preacher. He knew who to step to so let me make that clear. I know two people who backed him down for a fact.

I bet if Preacher walked out today and walked up and down 8th Avenue a lot of you wouldn't be going so hard like you do with others. Why is that? I'm listening. I would love to see you call him a Snitch to his face or on Social Media. It's amazing who people pick and choose who they shout out and talk bad about. It would be refreshing to see you keep up that same energy when it comes to everyone. I'm just saying.

Take a lesson from this story. Preacher was one of the strongest men in the streets of Harlem, yet he turned out to be one of the weakest. What he did can happen to you as well. Stop thinking it can't happen to you.

**THINK ABOUT IT!!**

# REAL SHIT

THIS IS ONE of the realest stories I've heard. The names have been changed to protect all parties.

A Spanish man named Chico and his best friend did business together in the streets. They were allegedly part of a gang as well. Chico and his friend Sammy ended up catching a case and going to prison. Sammy ended up snitching and Chico got 50 years in prison.

The word had spread that Sammy snitched and one day some guys jumped him and stabbed him for snitching on Chico. They hurt Sammy bad thinking that this is what Chico would have wanted and according to the unwritten rule snitches are supposed to get what's coming to them. Right?

Well the guys that had hurt Sammy came to Chico all happy thinking they were going to get a pat on their backs and expecting accolades for the work that they put in. They were so wrong about that. Chico ended up almost killing one of the dudes for what they had done to Sammy. Chico still considered Sammy his dear friend. Chico didn't blame Sammy for snitching; he blamed himself. Why you ask?

**Now this is the realest shit I've ever heard and it's so true.**

Chico said that he should have known better than to have Sammy down with him. He said that he knew what Sammy was and wasn't built for. Chico blamed NO ONE, but HIMSELF. Let this marinate for a minute... He accepted the 50 years and felt no way about what Sammy did.

Whether you were in the streets or not we have all dealt with someone who we knew wasn't the type who would fight or speak up when something went down. Females always had somebody in their crew who they knew was only good for holding the pocketbooks when shit was about to jump off. We knew she wasn't going to fight, and she wasn't expected to say a word. Dudes always had someone that was just good for holding and hiding the guns and work. They knew who was and who wasn't going to bust one shot as well as would be the one ducking and hiding when chaos jumped off.

I don't care what no one thinks. I give it up to Chico for not placing the blame on Sammy. Chico knew Sammy wasn't built for the streets like that. Sammy was his friend and Chico took full responsibility for the decision that Sammy made. Again, Chico took full responsibility for the decision that Sammy made.

This should be a lesson for those of you that are still *"about that life"*. Know who's around you. You must be satisfied with whatever decisions you make especially when the end result is not in your favor. You must take full responsibility for putting people in positions that they are not equipped for. Plain and Simple.

No matter what type of business you're running, it is your responsibility to have people that are responsible and will hold themselves accountable for what goes wrong. This is why most businesses have managers and supervisors that are trustworthy. People have to earn these high positions that they are given. Either legal or illegal it never made a difference. Business is business.

Again- Who made the rules? Chico knew that the game wasn't fair and that everybody was not built to play. I respect Chico. This story is not for those wannabe gangsters that run around hustling and busting your gun randomly hitting no one or innocent people and then turn around and tuck your penis when the cops come and then start snitching. Nope, you will not justify your ratty behavior based off of my writings.

Be conscious of who's around you and the responsibilities you bestow upon them.

# TEKASHI 6IX9INE

I F THE STORY is true about his so-called friends and employees, then how could anyone judge the decision this young man made. I see nothing wrong with what he needed to do to help himself. I don't see anything wrong with doing someone dirty, especially after knowing that they were planning to do it to you.

The story is that the Feds allowed this young rapper to hear taped recordings of his so-called friends and employees allegedly talking about him and planning to "**do him dirty**". This young man had already been kidnapped, beaten and robbed before all the arrests had occurred. Come to find out his own people set it up allegedly.

Only a fool, a follower of "the streets", and an idiot would say "He still should have held it down." Really? He had every right to do what he did after hearing what he heard and knowing that it was his own people who robbed him in that attack and was planning on doing something even worse to him. Tekashi was the reason they were eating. He was the reason anyone noticed them. He was the reason they were getting all the girls. They were riding high off his notoriety. He was the reason for their "fame by association", yet they were the ones who were planning to "do him dirty".

You can say what you want. You can have your own opinion as well, but I stand by what I say. No one will never know if Tekashi would have held it down had these recordings never surfaced. No one would never know if he's really a stand-up guy. What we do know is that his so-called friends and employees didn't hold him down. They allegedly stole from him. They allegedly messed with his girlfriend. They allegedly kidnapped, beat and robbed him. I say allegedly, but we all know what it is.

His own people failed to hold it down for him. The same people who were hired to protect him, book shows for him, pay him his money and "keep it real", were the same people who robbed and harmed him. Seriously, would you keep it real and hold it down if it were you?

Some of y'all rappers out here talking about how disappointed you are with him. GTFOH!!! With all of that. His own people tried to kill him, robbed him and violated him. It's really amazing to see how many people who have something to say about someone else's experience. Until you go through it, you don't have the right to have an opinion about how someone else should go about dealing with an experience such as his. Just my opinion.

Tekashi must understand that now he must change his behavior. His behavior in the past may the reason for how he was treated but is does not negate the fact that he was taken advantage of and treated poorly by his team. I wish him all the best. I hope he comes out, does lots of shows and makes a ton of money. Just my opinion.

# YOU JUST NEVER KNOW

THIS STORY HERE doesn't surprise me. I was just told this story recently. A good friend of mine named "Farrar" was doing a 40-year bid in the state and was brought down to the federal building at MCC back around 1995 for another case. "Farrar" was in a cell when this guy from Harlem was escorted in. The guy was like 6'5 and about 350 pounds back then. This guy had just been arrested in a big drug and murder sting. He was a very dangerous guy known in Harlem. He was allegedly killing up everything.

When the big guy enters the cell he begins to say to "Farrar",

*"Yo what's up with all those bodies from back in the 80's"* Says the guy.

*"Farrar" says, "What bodies are you talking about?"*

The big dude tries to go in and explain the bodies that he's referring to. In the meantime, "Farrar's" mind is going crazy trying to figure out why they brought him down to MCC as well as how this dude coincidentally became his celly. SET UP!!!!

While the big homie is running his mouth, "Farrar" says fuck it and takes his chances with the big dude and leaps on him. Now "Farrar" already knew he had no wins with the big guy, but his intentions were to get to the wires that he knew were hiding under homies shirt. As they fought "Farrar" grabbed homies shirt trying to pull it over his head and low and behold the wire was there. The big dude was trying to get "Farrar" on tape talking about some old bodies from the 80's.

Now listen, the big homie at one time was respected in the streets and was very well known for being a force to reckon with. He allegedly killed a lot of people himself. He was a guy that was arrested with one of the most dangerous crews from Harlem. Now "Farrar" was a contract killer back in the 70's and 80's. He had Harlem shook. From what he and others told me; when people saw him coming, they were closing up shop and getting out the way. So they both were about their business.

Now the big dude should have stood tall. He and Farrar never did business together so why the hell would he consider doing this to someone he had no business dealings with. Instead he took his chances trying to set someone up that was already doing a 40-year bid. This is what the streets and the game have come to. The game of who can set who up and get out of jail fast. It's hard being a black man in the streets all across the board. So, do you want to take these kinds of chances? The streets are fair game, but the game has never been fair. **THINK ABOUT IT!!**

# HONOR UP

LET ME SAY this. Some of you dudes that's screaming Honor up, wearing shirts, all up on the gram and in the videos (Suge Knight Voice) STOP IT! Some of you are not honorable. In your defense some of you may not even know it until things get thick.

A lot of "wannabe" gangsters have yet to be tested that's why you're running around calling everybody else a snitch or yelling out how honorable you are. But deep down in the pit of your stomach you know that you can't handle that smoke if it comes your way. And that's okay but stop the bullshit. Ms. Tee says it's okay to just be a regular dude that's not about that life. Regular dudes can still hang out with the gangsters and laugh and joke around. You can still be honorable outside of the "gangster life". This way when things jumps off, you're not really expected to do anything because everyone knows you're not about that life. For you pretenders, it's not a good look when you're standing there looking stupid because you were expected to participate, but was too scared to do so. You can't pick and choose when to be gangster. You either are or aren't.

I know a few honorable dudes who of course didn't want to do any time in prison, but they accepted their wrongs and did their time for it. Who wants to leave their wives and children behind? When you choose the game and the lifestyle you also chose to be honorable at that same time because that is what the game expects from you. Right? Only when that smoke comes, is when some dudes change the rules of the game. Again- **Who made the rules?**

HONORABLE is being a productive citizen of society and teaching your children the opposite of where you went wrong. Teaching your kids to be better than you is the most honorable thing you can do. Stepping your game up by educating yourself and leaving the streets behind is honorable. Not worrying about who snitched and who didn't is honorable. Who are we to judge? The game has never been fair There is no rule book. There are no codes. The game never came with guidelines to follow. If one lives a life without crime, then there would be no need to worry about this subject at all.

Stop listening to all these uneducated "BIG HOMIES" who still want to walk around with the same mindset of 25 years ago. **GROWTH** is more honorable and gangsta' than anything.

So, who has the real HONOR out in these streets? **THINK ABOUT IT!!!**

# 2019

I KEEP HAVING THE same conversation with a friend of mine because he can't seem to understand that snitching has become the norm. He's old school and he has and will always stand his ground and take his as it comes, but everybody is not like him. Snitching in 2019 is not surprising to me. I expect it to keep happening. It will continue to come from those we least expect as well.

April of 2019 2 guys that I know took the stand while everybody from the neighborhood sat in a Federal court room and watched. They had been locked down since late 2016 or earlier 2017. Now I will say this from experience; when someone is arrested by the Feds and taken to MCC, their stay should not take years. If someone you know has been arrested and they have been in MCC for over a year, there is a huge chance that they are cooperating. It makes no sense to be in MCC for one to two years claiming that you're holding out or waiting on a court date. No, most likely someone is cooperating. Just my experience.

From what I was told these two gentlemen took the stand telling on any and every one that they could think of. I wasn't shocked to hear about one of the guys because rumors had been swirling about him for years. The other not only surprised me, but it bothered me somewhat. He and I were cool, and his mother is a longtime friend of mine. From my understanding he did what he did to avoid doing ten years. If you can't do 5 to 10 years in prison for doing what you know is wrong, **GET OUT THE GAME**. That's nothing compared to someone facing life and the death penalty. If you men out here can't do ten years for being in the game and slipping up, then it's time to find another profession.

Another argument that I keep having with my friend is that everybody cannot and will not stand tall when they are expected to do so. That is the bottom line and the writing is on the paper literally. You never know who you are dealing with until the shit hits the fan. My question to all the men that are still in the street game is this- Why wait to test another man's loyalty? Why would you trust someone with your life? Why would you stand around yelling *"Nah he won't do that to me, that's family"*. I laugh and shake my head at your stupidity. Trust me it's every man for themselves. It's always been this way. This is nothing new, it's been happening for centuries. The streets are fair game, but the game has never been fair.

If and when it does happen, it's on you. When you leave your wife and kids, it's on you. When your man takes the stand on you, it's on you. When you are doing 30 years or life in prison that's on you. You might be saying to yourself that I sound crazy. No, I don't. If it's raining out, you take an umbrella. If it's snowing out, you dress appropriately. If you go to the gym you would wear sneakers and not shoes. If you can prepare for the gym and the climate like I stated above, why wouldn't you prepare for the climate of the streets now in 2019. The climate is not only hot or cold. The climate in the streets these days is that it's every man for themselves. Why not have more concern for your life and your family situation? Why not be prepared?

At the end of the day the street game isn't fair. Selling drugs and committing other crimes is still illegal. So, why not change the narrative of how your life will turn out. Having a job has never hurt anyone. There are so many other ways to make money and there is nothing corny about doing it the right way.

**THINK ABOUT IT!!**

# WHAT I LEARNED

A FTER TALKING TO several people and listening to their personal situations as well as watching my life over and over in my head, my opinion is that none of it is or ever was worth it. Death, betrayal, heartbreak, destruction of family and communities are the things that the lifestyle that we all wanted so bad has caused.

**RULES**- Well from what I have seen and gone thru over the course of my 33-year run in these streets, there are none. Let's forget about snitching for a minute.... If there were rules a lot of fallen soldiers would be standing. If there were rules a family member would not have set me up to be robbed while I was pregnant. If there were rules the next man wouldn't be fucking your wife while you're locked up. If there were rules your man would take care of you your whole bid. If there were rules people would kindly wait their turn instead of killing, betraying and destroying to take your spot.

The game was never made to be fair. The streets don't love you back. The first title of this book was **"Snitching- The Rise and Fall of the Game"**. I used the word "game" a few times in this book, but then I was checked and realized that it was a lifestyle that we chose. It was not a game. After several conversations a good friend said this to me:

**I'm very happy for you young lady and I do wish you the very best being not only my home girl from the city but comrade in arms, one thing I will respectfully disagree though is in the usage of the word "game" when referencing the drug business because this isn't no game, the killing the jail time the betrayal the Machiavellian**

**tactics, by no means is this a game, no time out's here baby just light's out. have a good night, respectfully, BG aka George "Boy George" Rivera.**

That's some real shit right there.

*Respectfully, Ms. Tee*

 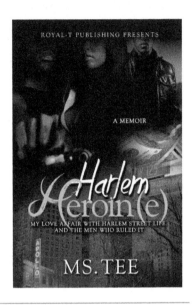

POUND GAME $15.00 +$4.00 S/H     HARLEM HEROIN(E) $11.99 + $4.00 S/H

INMATE NAME & NUMBER_____

ADDRESS_____

TITLE(S)_____

---

Cashier's Checks, Institutional Checks & Money Orders are acceptable

Make Payable To: ROYAL-T PUBLISHING, LLC
                 PO BOX 600
                 NY, NY 10030

PayPal@  Royaltypub@gmail.com

         www.msteebooks.net

Quantity:_____     Amount Enclosed:_____

# SNITCHING

## GUIDE TO HOW IT GOES DOWN

# MS. TEE

ROYAL-T
PUBLISHING